FOREST BOO

Only When the Messengers Come

OLLY KOMENDA-SOENTGERATH was born in Prague into a German family on the 23rd of October, 1923. She studied History and German at the famous Charles University. Her early poems and short stories were published in the 'Prager Tagblatt' ('Prague Daily News').

Since 1946 she has lived in the Federal Republic of Germany where, as a result of her personal circumstances, she began publishing her work relatively late. In 1982 she translated the poetry of Jaroslav Seifert, who in 1984 received the Nobel Prize for Literature. Seifert in turn translated Olly Komenda-Soentgerath's poetry into Czech. Three volumes of her poetry were published in Prague.

Olly Komenda-Soentgerath's poems have also been published in numerous anthologies, newspapers and magazines, as well as being broadcast on both radio and television. Her poetry has been set to music (subsequently recorded), and translated into a number of languages. – She is a member of the PEN-club and has been awarded various literary prizes, including the 'GEDOK Prize for Lyric Poetry' and the 'Culture Prize for Literature', endowed by the Free State of Bavaria. Her poems were first published in the UK in the volume *Under My Eyelids* (Forest, 1994).

TOM BECK was born in London in 1941. After studying Music and English at the universities of Birmingham and Oxford, he was for a time the London arts correspondent of the *Frankfurter Allgemeine Zeitung*. He also produced a number of studies of various aspects of twentieth-century music. In 1970 he moved permanently to West Germany, where he taught Music and English at both a *Gymnasium* and at university. He gave many public lecture-workshops on music with the pianist Bernhard Wambach, as well as broadcasting on West German radio. Since 1984 he has been collaborating with the German poet-singer, Wolf Biermann, on a translation of his poetry and prose.

Returning to Britain in 1991, he now works as a translator, and has translated plays by Wolfgang-Maria Bauer and Harald Kislinger for the Royal Court Theatre, and poetry by Goethe, Heine and Rilke.

Olly Komenda-Soentgerath

Only When the Messengers Come

Poems by
Olly Komenda-Soentgerath

Translated from the German by
Tom Beck

FOREST BOOKS
London & Boston

PUBLISHED BY
FOREST BOOKS

20 Forest View, Chingford, London E3 7AY, UK
P.O. Box 312, Lincoln Centre, MA 01773, USA

First published 1995

Typeset in Great Britain by Fleetlines Typesetters, Southend-on-Sea
Printed in Great Britain by BPC Wheatons Ltd, Exeter

Original Poems ©Olly Komenda-Soentgerath
Translations © Tom Beck
Cover design © Ian Evans

ALL RIGHTS RESERVED

A CIP catalogue record for this book is available from
the British Library

ISBN 1-85610-040-5

Library of Congress Catalogue Card No:
95–60234

The original German poems were published in 1992 by Heiderhoff Verlag, Eisingen, in the volume entitled ERST WENN DIE BOTEN KOMMEN. Forest is grateful to Heiderhoff Verlag for the right to reproduce these poems in this dual text edition.

Contents

I. A DANGEROUS GAME

Everything is in Order	10
Es ist alles in Ordnung	11
Hoarfrost	12
Rauhreif	13
Winter	12
Winter	13
Benumbed, No	14
Erstarren, nein	15
Laws of Gravity	14
Fallgesetz	15
Crystal Words	16
Gläserne Worte	17
Guitar	16
Gitarre	17
When	18
Wenn	19
Differently	18
Anders	19
Wordless	20
Wortlos	21
A Dangerous Game	22
Gefährliches Spiel	23
Conditional Mood	24
Möglichkeitsform	25
Room for Life	26
Platz fur Leben	27
Adam and Eve	28
Adam und Eva	29
Interpreter	30
Dolmetscher	31

II. WITHOUT A USE-BY DATE

In old Age	34
Im Alter	35
Horizon	36
Horizont	37
Evening	38
Der Abend	39
The Old-New Song	38
Das altneue Lied	39
The River	40
Der Fluß	41
Subterranean	40
Unterirdisch	41
Old Man	42
Der alte Mann	43
Tree in Winter	42
Baum im Winter	43
September	44
September	45
Mollusc-Shell	44
Muschelschale	45
Sunset	46
Sonnenuntergang	47
Tortoise I	48
Schildkröte I	49
Tortoise II	48
Schildkröte II	49
Gaudy Summer I	50
Bunter Sommer I	51
Rainy Summer II	52
Verregneter Sommer II	53
Farewell	52
Abschied	53

Reserves   54
  Vorrat   55
Without a Use-By Date   54
  Ohne Verfallsdatum   55
Being at Home   56
  Zu Hause sein   57
Game   58
  Spiel   59
Rainbow   60
  Regenbogen   61
Old Woman   60
  Die Greisin   61
Restless   62
  Rastlos   63
Awakening   62
  Erwachen   63
Rubbed Out   64
  Ausradiert   65

III. IN THE AUDITORIUM

Strike   68
  Streik   69
Only a Film   70
  Ein Film nur   71
Sometime   70
  Irgendwann   71
Applause   72
  Beifall   73
Poet   72
  Dichter   73
Dance of the Veils   74
  Schleiertanz   75

Cloister	74
Kloster	75
The Law of Chance	76
Das Gesetz des Zufalls	77
Leavings	76
Zurückgeblieben	77
Prague *Kleinseite* at Night	78
Prager Kleinseite bei Nacht	79
Pram	78
Kinderwagen	79
Souvenir from Prague	80
Souvenir aus Prag	81
In the Auditorium	82
Im Zuschauerraum	83
Week's End	84
Wochen-Ende	85
Christopher C.	84
Christoph K.	85
Reminiscence	86
Erinnerung	87
Kismet, He Says	86
Kismet, sagt er	87

IV. IN THE BEGINNING WAS THE DREAM

Cemetery by the Sea	90
Friedhof am Meer	91
Creation	90
Schöpfung	91
Unknown	92
Unbekannt	93
Giving Notice	92
Kündigung	93

Cain and Abel	94
Kain und Abel	95
That is the End of the News	94
Ende der Nachrichten	95
Without a Parachute	96
Ohne Fallschirm	97
Future Without a Future	96
Zukunft ohne Zukunft	97
Existence	98
Das Sein	99
More than Anything	98
Mehr als alles	99
The Final Moment	100
Der jüngste Augenblick	101
The Third Commandment	100
Das dritte Gebot	101
In the Beginning was the Dream	102
Im Anfang war der Traum	103
Primaeval Time	102
Ur-Zeit	103
Going Back	104
Zurück	105
Presentiment	104
Ahnung	105
Typhoon	106
Taifun	107
Asylum Seekers	106
Asylanten	107
Death, My Friend	108
Tod, mein Freund	109
Not Entirely	110
Nicht ganz	111

Blackboard	110
Die Tafel	111
Dead Death	112
Der tote Tod	113
On the Styx	112
Am Styx	113
My Star	114
Mein Stern	115

V. SMOKE SIGNALS

Metamorphosis	118
Metamorphose	119
Photo	118
Foto	119
The Book	120
Das Buch	121
Obituary	120
Nachruf	121
Computer Guided	122
Computergesteuert	123
The Idea	122
Die Idee	123
Discussion Circle	124
Diskussionsrunde	125
Career	124
Karriere	125
Smoke Signals	126
Rauchzeichen	127
Who?	126
Wer?	127
Reason	128
Ratio	129
A Face	128

Ein Gesicht	129
Scepticism	130
Skepsis	131
Engaged	130
Besetzt	131
We	132
Wir	133
Winged Snail	132
Flügelschnecke	133
No Difference	134
Kein Unterschied	135
Sisyphus	134
Sisyphus	135
Freedom	136
Freiheit	137
Put on Ice	136
Auf Eis gelegt	137

A Dangerous Game

Everything is in Order

You meet me halfway.
You know your lines
and I know
my answer.

This is no first night.
These boards
and the heavens
of the gridiron
are so very familiar to us.

Why then the fear
that we might no longer
recognize each other
in different lighting?

Everything is in order.

Es ist alles in Ordnung

Du kommst mir entgegen,
dein Text ist bekannt,
und bekannt ist
meine Antwort.

Das ist keine Premiere.
Diese Bretter
und der Himmel
des Schnürbodens
sind uns vertraut.

Warum die Angst,
wir könnten einander
bei veränderter Beleuchtung
nicht mehr erkennen?

Es ist alles in Ordnung.

Hoarfrost

Hoarfrost
on the pavement
before my window.
Hoarfrost
interwoven
with pigtails
of birds' footprints,
four-pointed.

No trace
of shoe-size 43.

Only birds' footprints.
four-pointed.

Winter

It has surpassed itself.

Whiter than white,
colder than cold,
more dead than dead.

And yet your breath
dances in the air,
alive, warm and close.

Rauhreif

Rauhreif
am Bürgersteig
vor meinem Fenster.
Rauhreif
durchflochten
von Zöpfen
aus Vogelfußstapfen,
viergezackt.

Keine Spur
von Schuhgröße 43.

Nur Vogelfußstapfen,
viergezackt.

Winter

Er hat sich übertroffen.

Weißer als weiß,
kälter als kalt,
toter als tot.

Doch in der Luft
tanzt dein Atem
lebendig, warm und nah.

Benumbed, No

Be still, he says.
And do not move!

Love is high
above us
at its zenith.
Each further step
could give birth to shadows.

She laughs and
dancing, pulls him
away with her.

Laws of Gravity

Birds do not fly
in airless space.
You know that.

Your twofold breath
has carried my wings
high over
mountain- and tree-tops.

Your rallentando
has left me quite
thunderstruck.

The earth now has me once again.

Erstarren, nein

Bleib stehn, sagt er.
Beweg dich nicht!

Die Liebe steht
hoch über uns
im Zenit.
Jeder weitere Schritt
könnte Schatten gebären.

Sie lacht und
zieht ihn tanzend
mit sich fort.

Fallgesetz

Vögel fliegen nicht
im luftleeren Raum.
Das weißt du.

Dein doppelter Atem
trug meine Flügel
hoch über
Wipfel und Gipfel.

Dein Rallentando
ließ mich aus
allen Wolken fallen.

Die Erde hat mich wieder.

Crystal Words

With crystal words
we have
drunk
to our happiness.

Were our hands
too ardent?
Or the happiness
too stormy?

The fragments
stutter on the floor.

Guitar

You haven't gone,
you haven't really slipped away,
you have just hidden
yourself within your
guitar.

Sometimes in the evening
when the darkness
rises from its body,
sometimes in the evening
between piano
and pianissimo
I hear your song.

Gläserne Worte

Wir haben
mit gläsernen Worten
angestoßen
auf unser Glück.

Waren unsere Hände
zu heftig?
Oder zu stürmisch
das Glück?

Die Scherben
stammeln am Boden.

Gitarre

Du bist nicht gegangen,
du bist nicht fort,
du hast dich
in deiner Gitarre
versteckt.

Manchmal am Abend,
wenn das Dunkel
aus ihrem Körper steigt,
manchmal am Abend
zwischen piano
und pianissimo
hör ich dich singen.

When

When you are nowhere near me

my eyes paint you
in colour and light;

my hands fumble
for your contours,

my words follow
echoes of yours,

my thoughts
replenish and complete you.

When you are nowhere near me
you are yet so close to me.

Differently

Move your tenderness
from your fingertips
into your eyes.

Move your tenderness
from the palm of your hand
into your smile.

Move your tenderness
from your arms
into your whispers.

Be tenderness itself to me.

Wenn

Wenn du nicht bei mir bist,

malen dich meine Augen
in Farbe und Licht,

meine Hände testen
nach deinen Konturen,

meine Worte folgen
dem Echo der deinen,

meine Gedanken
füllen dich an und aus.

Wenn du nicht bei mir bist,
bist du bei mir.

Anders

Leg deine Zärtlichkeit
aus den Fingerkuppen
in deine Augen.

Leg deine Zärtlichkeit
aus den Handflächen
in dein Lächeln.

Leg deine Zärtlichkeit
aus den Armen
in dein Flüstern.

Sei zärtlich zu mir.

Wordless

She speaks only Czech.
But all that she says
is Greek
to him.

He comes from Amsterdam.
And what he says
seems to her a little like
double Dutch.

She smiles at him.
He smiles back.

Can you understand
how these two
understand each other so well?

Wortlos

Sie spricht nur tschechisch.
Was sie erzählt,
sind böhmische Dörfer
für ihn.

Er stammt aus Madrid.
Was er ihr sagt,
kommt ihr ein wenig
spanisch vor.

Sie lächelt ihn an.
Er lächelt zurück.

Verstehst du,
daß die beiden
sich so gut verstehen?

A Dangerous Game

My envoys,
white pebbles,
caper
to you
across the water.

Your envoys,
white spinning tops,
gambol
to me
across the waves.

Between seashore
and seashore
exultation
at the contact.

Between seashore
and seashore
a scream
when they fall.

Gefährliches Spiel

Meine Boten,
weiße Kiesel,
hüpfen
über das Wasser
hinüber zu dir.

Deine Boten,
Kiesel in Weiß,
springen
über die Wellen
herüber zu mir.

Zwischen Ufer
und Ufer
ein Jauchzen
bei der Berührung.

Zwischen Ufer
und Ufer
beim Absturz
ein Schrei.

Conditional Mood

To love
in the subjunctive.
What would happen, if . . .

No,
no plunge
into an embrace
which would
be smothered
by the full stop.

Only
steps,
punctuated,
endless,
never arriving.
What would happen if . . .

Möglichkeitsform

Lieben
im Konjunktiv.
Was wäre, wenn ...

Nein,
kein Sturz
in eine Umarmung,
die vom Schlußpunkt
erdrückt wird.

Nur
Schritte,
punktiert,
endlos,
ohne Ankunft.
Was wäre, wenn ...

Room for Life

Throw the anxiety
from your eyes
into mine!
I will
out-fear it
for you.

And lay the trembling of your hands
upon my skin.
The tremble will fade away.

Let me scream
your scream.
which thrusts
the smile from your lips,

and die
your many deaths,
one after the other,

until there is room
in your veins
for life.

Platz fur Leben

Wirf die Angst
aus deinen Augen
in die meinen!
Durchfürchten
will ich sie
für dich.

Das Zittern deiner Hände
leg auf meine Haut.
Es wird verebben.

Schreien laß mich
deinen Schrei,
der dir das Lächeln
von den Lippen stößt,

und sterben
deine vielen Tode,
einen nach dem anderen,

bis Platz
in deinen Adern wird
für Leben.

Adam and Eve
(For Paul Konrad Kurz)

And then,
Oh Lord, when I begged you,
to grant me a companion
you wrenched a piece
out of me.
You have destroyed
my entirety.
I have searched
since then for my
missing part,
and my missing part
has searched for me.

Once in a thousand years
you join us together again,
once in a thousand years
we plunge into each other
in eternal happiness.

Oh, but this eternity lasts
merely for a moment.
In the next I roam around
for a thousand years
and search and search.

Adam und Eva
(Für Paul Konrad Kurz)

Damals,
als ich dich bat, mein Herr,
mir eine Gefährtin zu geben,
hast du ein Stück
herausgerissen aus mir.
Meine Ganzheit
hast du zerstört.
Seither such ich
mein fehlendes Teil,
und mein fehlendes Teil
sucht mich.

Einmal in tausend Jahren
fügst du uns wieder zusammen.
Einmal in tausend Jahren
stürzen wir ineinander
im ewigen Glück.

Ach, diese Ewigkeit dauert
einen Augenblick nur.
Im nächsten irre ich
tausend Jahre umher
und suche und suche.

Interpreter

He repeats
clever sentences
in four languages,
perfectly.

But in none
can he think.

He repeats
flattering words
in four languages.

In none
can he love.

Dolmetscher

In vier Sprachen
wiederholt er
kluge Sätze,
perfekt.

In keiner
kann er denken.

In vier Sprachen
wiederholt er
Schmeichelworte,
perfekt.

In keiner
kann er lieben.

Without a Use-by Date

In Old Age

Now things move faster.

With redoubled breath
the wind turns
over
the days.
Too hastily
for exhausted eyes.
The inscription
remains unread.
Having become tired,
the thoughts stay
at home.
They no longer
cast a shadow.
Behind the lattice cross
of the window
they vary
the sound
of a book slammed shut.

Im Alter

Jetzt geht es schneller.

Mit doppeltem Atem
blättert der Wind
die Tage um.
Zu hastig
für verbrauchte Augen.
Die Inschrift
bleibt ungelesen.
Müde geworden,
hocken die Gedanken
zu Hause.
Sie werfen
keine Schatten mehr.
Hinter dem Gitterkreuz
des Fensters
variieren sie
das Geräusch
eines zuschlagenden Buches.

Horizon

You
my horizon
which I

move towards
run towards
live towards

you beckon to me
smile

and

withdraw
with the speed
of my approaching
step

Horizont

Du
mein Horizont
dem ich

entgegengehe
entgegenlaufe
entgegenlebe

du winkst mir zu
lächelst

und

ziehst dich zurück
mit der Geschwindigkeit
meines näherkommenden
Schritts

Evening

In the frame of the door
stands the evening.

Half its face
speaks of the day.
Half its face
sings of the stars.

It has
chosen
song.

The Old-New Song

Composed
by the forest

conducted
by branches

sung
by birds

danced
by the wind

the old-new song

Der Abend

Im Rahmen der Tür
steht der Abend.

Die Hälfte seines Gesichts
erzählt vom Tage.
Die Hälfte seines Gesichts
singt von den Sternen.

Er hat sich
für den Gesang
entschieden.

Das altneue Lied

Komponiert
vom Wald

dirigiert
von Zweigen

gesungen
von Vögeln

getanzt
vom Wind

das altneue Lied

The River

Between mountains
and planes
the river
searching
for the sea.

Explorers,
ascended from its streaming body,
signal the direction
to it
from the perspective
of the sky.

Subterranean

Skulls
without tongues
speak of
that which
once was.

Roots
without leaves
whisper
of that which
will be.

Der Fluß

Der Fluß
zwischen Bergen
und Ebenen
auf der Suche
nach dem Meer.

Kundschafter,
aufgestiegen
aus seinem strömenden Leib,
signalisieren ihm
aus der Himmelsperspektive
die Richtung.

Unterirdisch

Schädel
zungenlos
erzählen
von dem
was war

Wurzeln
blätterlos
flüstern
von dem
was wird

Old Man

The weight of time
squats upon his back.
Departed days and nights.
nest in the engravings
of his face.
His shoes scrape
above the ground,
hardly a foot
from the end.

Yet the puffs of smoke
from his pipe signal:
I am still here.

Tree in Winter

The breathing finery
fallen away with the light

the denuded skeleton

Snake-dance
frozen in death

black metaphor
on the horizon

Der alte Mann

Die Schwere der Zeit
hockt auf seinem Rücken.
In den Gravuren
seines Gesichts nisten
gewesene Tage und Nächte.
Seine Schuhe kratzen
über dem Boden
einen fußbreit
vom Ende.

Aber die Rauchzeichen
seiner Pfeife signalisieren:
Noch bin ich.

Baum im Winter

Der atmende Schmuck
abgefallen mit dem Licht

nackt das Skelett

Schlangentanz
erstarrt im Tode

schwarze Metapher
am Horizont

September

Bedewed spiders' webs
between drowsy leaves.

Swansong of light
sparkling once more
in diamond-brilliant
fragmentation.

Did the air just sigh?

Behind the hills
the storms of the night
are already collecting.

Mollusc-Shell

Mollusc-shell,
half opened lips
rigid in
the scream of death.
Supplicant duration murmurs
on and on
in armour
become useless,
the lullaby
of swaying seaweed.

September

Betaute Spinnennetze
zwischen müden Blättern.

Abgesang des Lichts
einmal noch aufglühend
in diamantener
Zersplitterung.

Seufzte die Luft?

Hinter den Hügeln
sammeln sich schon
die Stürme der Nacht.

Muschelschale

Muschelschale,
halbgeöffnete Lippen,
erstarrt im
Aufschrei des Todes.
Erflehte Dauer rauscht
im sinnlos
gewordenen Panzer
fort und fort
das Wiegenlied
schaukelnden Tangs.

Sunset

This is how the great die.

The day
has long known
of the departure.
The skies have
silently gathered
for the parting
to receive
the final effusion.
The carpet of the sea
lays itself
beneath the florid
lavishness of light.

When it is over
the lustre
above the grave
will long retell it.

Sonnenuntergang

So sterben Große.

Lange schon
weiß der Tag
von dem Abschied.
Der Himmel
versammelt sich still
bei der Sinkenden,
um ihr letztes Verströmen
zu empfangen.
Der Teppich des Meeres
legt sich
unter die bunte
Verschwendung des Lichts.

Wenn sie gegangen ist,
wird die Helle
über dem Grab
lange von ihr erzählen.

Tortoise I

To be a tortoise,
draw in
head and legs
beneath the shell.

Lie motionless,
a stone
among stones.

Tortoise II

The tortoise
exchanged
its 300
sleepy years

for
the 3,
filled with vivacity,
allotted to
the wren,

which has never regretted
its life
without noughts.

Schildkröte I

Schildkröte sein,
Kopf und Beine
einziehen
unter den Panzer.

Reglos liegen,
ein Stein
zwischen Steinen.

Schildkröte II

Die Schildkröte
tauschte
ihre 300
schläfrigen Jahre

gegen
die 3
voll Lebendigkeit,
die dem Zaunkönig
zugeteilt waren.

Sie hat nicht bereut,
ohne Nullen
zu leben.

Gaudy Summer I

Sunflowers
have rolled
the summer
into the gardens.
Yellow spokes
disseminate the smile
of their namesake.

The church tower
in rococo white
peals out the news
from its throat
over alleys and roofs.

Down there the poplars
between the fields
have understood.
They paint
the greeting
with green brushes
back into the azure.

Bunter Sommer I

Sonnenblumen
haben den Sommer
in die Gärten gerollt.
Gelbe Speichen
verbreiten das Lächeln
ihrer Namenspatronin.

Der Kirchturm,
in Rokoko-Weiß,
läutet die Nachricht
aus seinem Hals
über Dächer und Gassen.

Drüben, die Pappeln,
zwischen den Feldern,
haben verstanden.
Sie malen
mit grünen Pinseln
den Gruß
zurück in die Bläue.

Rainy Summer II

Summer
is not taking place.

Puddles expand.
Leaves, rain-heavy,
cement July
to November.

Yet in the branches
the rumour obdurately
continues, of something
which glows and warms.

Farewell

There were days
of emerald and topaz.
Blossoming smile.
And the Spring
believed the Spring.

The wind
now snuffles
along the kerbstones
under the husky leaves
after something
which should endure,
after something
that has gone.

Verregneter Sommer II

Der Sommer
findet nicht statt.

Pfützen wachsen.
Blätter, regenschwer,
kleben den Juli
an den November.

Doch in den Zweigen
hält sich hartnäckig
das Gerücht von etwas,
das leuchtet und wärmt.

Abschied

Tage gab es
aus Smaragd und Topas.
Aufblühendes Lächeln.
Der Frühling
glaubte dem Frühling.

Jetzt schnüffelt
der Wind
den Bordstein entlang
unter heiserem Laub
nach etwas,
das bleiben sollte,
nach etwas,
das ging.

Reserves

The battery of the pulse
loaded
by the noonday sun.

In the sea of flowers
refuelled with
breaths.

Reserves
for winter nights
in which it snows
loneliness.

Without a Use-By Date

To hold oneself tight
with both hands
on tufts of grass
which splinter stones.

With green stalks
heal up
the use-by date
of the earth.

Vorrat

Die Batterie des Pulses
an hoher Sonne
geladen.

Im Blumenmeer
Atemzüge
getankt.

Vorrat
für Winternächte,
in denen es
Einsamkeit schneit.

Ohne Verfallsdatum

Sich festhalten
mit beiden Händen
an Grasbüscheln,
die Steine spalten.

Mit grünen Halmen
zuwachsen
das Verfallsdatum
der Erde.

Being at Home
(For Hans Bender)

To have roots
deep in the blood
of the earth,

to say good morning
with leaf and twig
to the neighbouring bush,

to call the flowers
all around
in the meadow
by name

and know
where the sun
sets
in the evening.

Zu Hause sein
(Für Hans Bender)

Wurzeln haben
tief im Blut
der Erde,

mit Laub und Zweigen
Guten Morgen sagen
zu dem Nachbarstrauch,

alle Blumen
ringsum
in der Wiese
mit dem Namen
rufen

und wissen,
wo die Sonne
untergeht
am Abend.

Game

Clouds,
the team in white,
running
across a blue arena.

Shadows,
players in grey,
rushing
over the green field.

Applause and censure
twittering
from the grandstand
of twigs.

And all because of
a yellow ball.

Spiel

Wolken,
Mannschaft in Weiß,
laufen
über blaue Arena.

Schatten,
Spieler in Grau,
jagen
über grünes Feld.

Beifall und Kritik
zwitschert
von den Tribünen
der Zweige.

Es geht
um den gelben Ball.

Rainbow

To wander
beneath your
iridescent arch
into the vast lands
and distant
quite distant
enter into
the horizon

To ascend
on your radiant colours
above the earth
and high
so high
enter into
heaven

Old Woman

Fallen out,
the wisdom teeth
with their kith and kin.

An orphaned tooth,
the last one,
holds monologues
in a
sunken jaw.

Regenbogen

Unter deiner
bunten Wölbung
hineinwandern
ins weite Land
und fern
ganz fern
eingehen
in den Horizont

An deinen
leuchtenden Farben
aufsteigen
über die Erde
und hoch
ganz hoch
eingehen
in den Himmel

Die Greisin

Ausgefallen
die Weisheitszähne
und ihre Geschwister.

Der Waisenzahn,
der letzte,
hält Monologe
im eingefallenen Kiefer.

Restless

Bird, you
born without feet,
in restless flight
from day to night to day.
No twig on which to find repose.
Your shadow touches
only paths and roofs.

Finally only
in the plunge
your heart, flown empty,
between the green of the blades of grass.

Greeting and farewell.

Awakening

The day is young.
The day is full of curiosity.

It holds its
glowing torch
up high behind the darkness
along the mountain's back.

It wants to see
how the earth
awakes.

Rastlos

Vogel, du,
ohne Füße geboren,
in rastlosem Flug
vom Tag zur Nacht zum Tag.
Kein Zweig zum Ausruhen.
Wege und Dächer
berührt nur dein Schatten.

Zuletzt erst
im Absturz
dein leergeflogenes Herz
zwischen dem Grün der Halme.

Begrüßung und Abschied.

Erwachen

Der Tag ist jung.
Der Tag ist voll Neugier.

Er hält seine
leuchtende Fackel
hinter dem Dunkel
der Bergrücken hoch.

Sehen will er,
wie die Erde
erwacht.

Rubbed Out

With a white shell
I write
my name
in the sand.

The waves,
filled with curiosity,
lick at the letters
and playfully carry
the contours
bit by bit
on their backs
off to a
distant adventure.

What remains
in the bay
is the nameless sand,
damp and smooth.

Ausradiert

Mit weißer Muschel
schreib ich
meinen Namen
in den Sand.

Die Wellen lecken
voller Neugier
an den Lettern
und tragen übermütig
die Konturen
Stück für Stück
auf ihrem Rücken
zu einem
fernen Abenteuer.

Zurückgeblieben
in der Bucht
ist der namenlose Sand,
feucht und glatt.

In the Auditorium

Strike

They are on strike:
my arms and my legs,
my stomach, my heart.

They are rehearsing
a revolution against a lofty dictator,
the head.

All too long
has it
incited,
whipped
and pursued.

The brain was doubtless
not brainy enough.
It has overrated
its strength.

Now its subjects
are on strike.

I declare my
solidarity.
I too am on strike.

Streik

Sie streiken:
meine Arme und Beine,
mein Magen, mein Herz.

Sie proben den Aufstand
gegen den hohen Diktator,
den Kopf.

Allzulange
hat er sie
angetrieben,
gepeitscht,
gejagt.

Der Kluge war wohl
nicht klug genug.
Er hat seine Macht
überschätzt.

Jetzt streiken
die Untertanen.

Ich erkläre mich
solidarisch.
Ich streike mit.

Only a Film

You are the television screen,
we are the film.
Yours is the text,
we merely repeat it.
You direct,
we dance
your measure.
and when you call:
Lights out!
we become a film screen
within your film screen,
as if we had never existed.

Sometime

At sometime,
some days ago,
I lost my way, you see.
The wishes
and the questions,
I took them all with me.

The writing table.
the old wallpaper,
the curses and a prayer,
they have also gone with me.

But now I am able
to make a start
at the difficult part
of also doing
completely without – me.

Ein Film nur

Du bist der Bildschirm,
wir sind der Film.
Dein ist der Text,
wir sprechen ihn nach.
Du führst Regie,
wir tanzen
dein Taktmaß.
Und wenn du rufst:
Licht aus!
werden wir Leinwand,
in deiner Leinwand,
als wären wir nie gewesen.

Irgendwann

Irgendwann vor Tagen
bin ich mir
abhandengekommen.
Die Wünsche
und die Fragen
habe ich mitgenommen.

Der Schreibtisch,
die alte Tapete,
Flüche und Gebete
sind mitgegangen.

Jetzt hab ich
angefangen,
ohne mich
auszukommen.

Applause

The applause
leaves him
indifferent,
and with the catcalls
of the crowd
it is no different.

He says this
and cups his hand
to his ear
to hear even better.

Poet

Matrix
for the contour
of the contours.

Picture-writing
dictated
in a code of signs.

Then the impression
without anaesthetic:
sensuousness and pain.

Beifall

Gleichgültig
ist ihm der Beifall,
gleich ungültig
die Schmährufe
der Menge.

Er sagt es
und legt die Hand
hinter die Ohrmuschel,
um besser zu hören.

Dichter

Matrize
für die Kontur
der Konturen

Bildschrift
diktiert
im Code der Zeichen

Beim Eindruck
ohne Betäubung
Wollust und Schmerz

Dance of the Veils

The poem
a veiled dance

revealing
concealing

in the breeze
between which
words breathe

Cloister

In the centre of the atrium
the fountain talks
of unremembered times.

Confused by the stories,
the novice stumbles
over the lustre of light
between pillar and pillar.

Schleiertanz

Das Gedicht
ein Schleiertanz

enthüllend
verdeckend

im Luftzug
dazwischen
atmen Worte

Kloster

In der Mitte des Atriums
erzählt der Springbrunnen
von vergangenen Zeiten.

Verwirrt von den Geschichten
stolpert der Novize
über den Lichtschein
zwischen Säule und Säule.

The Law of Chance

I know the law
of chance.
It is corrupt.
It turns
to the cardinal points
of deepest longings.

I am holding
my compass needle
towards sunrise.

Leavings

What remains
of me
in Bangkok,
San Francisco and
here or there?

In the wastepaper basket
of the hotel room
a hank
of combed-out hair.

Das Gesetz des Zufalls

Ich kenne das Gesetz
des Zufalls.
Es ist bestechlich.
Es dreht sich
in die Himmelsrichtung
des tiefsten Wunsches.

Ich halte meine
Kompaßnadel
gegen Sonnenaufgang.

Zurückgeblieben

Was ist von mir
zurückgeblieben
in Bangkok,
San Francisco und
da und dort?

Im Papierkorb
des Hotelzimmers
ein Knäuel
ausgekämmter Haare.

Prague *Kleinseite* at Night

On the dome
of the Church of St. Nicholas
the green of the patina
scarcely lighter
than the moon.

Between the pillars
of leafy arcades
shadows of the centuries,
hardly darker
than the night.

On the banks
of the Moldau
ripples of dream,
a little deeper
than the sea.

(Kleinseite is a district of Prague)

Pram

She pushes
what will follow her
right on ahead.

Both present
and future
smile
at each other.

Prager *Kleinseite* bei Nacht

Auf der Kuppel
der Niklaskirche
das Grün der Patina
ein wenig heller
als der Mond

Zwischen den Säulen
der Laubengänge
Schatten der Jahrhunderte
ein wenig dunkler
als die Nacht

An den Ufern
der Moldau
Wellen aus Träumen
ein wenig tiefer
als das Meer

Kinderwagen

Sie schiebt,
was nach ihr kommt,
vor sich her.

Gegenwart
und Zukunft
lächeln einander
an.

Souvenir from Prague

No
not a postcard
of the Hradschin
of the Charles Bridge

only
in the photo album
my yellowing smile
under a tree
in the Rieger Park

in my ears
a hymn to the Virgin
sung by the
bells of the Church of Loreto

on my shoes
the dust
of Mount Zizka
which has never
been shaken off

in my hand
a handkerchief filled
with longings for home

Souvenir aus Prag

Nein
keine Ansichtskarte
vom Hradschin
und von der Karlsbrücke

nur
im Fotoalbum
mein vergilbtes Lächeln
unter einem Baum
des Riegerparks

in meinen Ohren
das Marienlied
gesungen von den
Glocken der Loretokirche

auf meinen Schuhen
der Staub vom Žižka-Berg
der niemals
abgeschüttelt wird

in meiner Hand
ein Taschentuch
voll Heimweh

In the Auditorium

Down there
in the auditorium
I sit
in the first row
silent and still.

Observe how,
up there
high on the stage,
I speak and sing,
laugh and dance,
weep and suffer.

An invisible
scene-shifter
changes pictures
and frames.

An invisible
make-up man
digs fold upon fold
in my face.

I, down there,
in the first row,
look on,
silent and still.

Im Zuschauerraum

Da unten
im Zuschauerraum
sitze ich
in der ersten Reihe
regungslos stumm.

Beobachte,
wie ich da oben
hoch auf der Bühne
spreche und singe,
lache und tanze,
weine und leide.

Unsichtbarer
Kulissenschieber
wechselt Bilder
und Rahmen.

Unsichtbarer
Maskenbildner
gräbt Falte um Falte
in mein Gesicht.

Ich, da unten,
in der ersten Reihe
schaue zu
regungslos stumm.

Week's End

Five days a week
fastened
to the telephone,
held together
with paper fasteners.

But the last two,
the very last,
what could *they*
hold on to?

Christopher C.

He sailed
after the sinking
sun,
searching
for the land
where it rose.

In between
the hindrance,
a world-transforming
mistake.

Wochen-Ende

Fünf Tage der Woche,
festgebunden
an den Telefonhörer,
zusammengehalten
mit Büroklammern.

Aber die letzten beiden,
die letzten,
wo sollen sie
sich anklammern?

Christoph K.

Nachgesegelt
der sinkenden
Sonne
auf der Suche
nach dem Land
ihres Aufgangs

Dazwischen
das Hindernis
ein weltverändernder
Irrtum

Reminiscence

Retouching
while rewinding
is allowed.

You send
the erosion only to such stones
as lie in your way
and you know
how to prevent
Fridays.

But you raise
the whispered word
of former times
with the aura
of the full moon.

Kismet, He Says

Who was it that wrote up my diary
before the start of my first day, then,
but now who knows what might happen to me
in the week's seven days, where and when?

The days, laid out like a railway track,
must be travelled along, no matter how tough,
for it's now up to me to get there and back:
I know I'm travelling, that's surely enough.

Erinnerung

Beim Zurückspulen
ist das Retuschieren
erlaubt.

Die Erosion
schickst du nur Steinen,
die im Wege liegen,
und Freitage
weißt du zu verhindern.

Aber das Flüsterwort
von damals
überhöhst du
mit der Aura
des vollen Mondes.

Kismet, sagt er

Wer hat mein Tagebuch geschrieben,
bevor mein erster Tag begann,
wer weiß, was mir in diesen sieben
der Woche zustößt, wo und wann?

Die Tage, ausgelegt als Gleise,
sind abzufahren, und es liegt
jetzt nicht an mir, ob diese Reise
gelingt. Ich fahre, das genügt.

In the Beginning Was the Dream

Cemetery by the Sea

The old cemetery
in Beaumont
looks out at the sea.

The faded writing
on the gravestone
whispers into the waves:
"Le temps qui passe
est le Dieux qui vient."

On the back
of wet furrows
time drifts towards
the horizon.

The heavens wait.

Creation

The unity split into single atoms,
and since then just war upon war:
of brains, of stars and chromosomes,
defeat out of triumph, and nothing more.

All that remains on elliptical ways
in spinning debris of the great explosion
is the undamaged kernel, just a trace
of a real return to some sort of fusion.

Friedhof am Meer

Der alte Friedhof
in Beaumont
schaut auf das Meer.

Die Schrift, verblaßt
am Grabstein,
flüstert in die Wellen:
»Le temps qui passe
est le Dieux qui vient.«

Auf dem Rücken
nasser Furchen
treibt die Zeit
zum Horizont.

Der Himmel wartet.

Schöpfung

Die Einheit gespalten in Ich-Atome,
damals. Und seither Krieg und Krieg:
der Gehirne, Gestirne, der Chromosome.
In Niederlagen zerfällt jeder Sieg.

Geblieben ist auf elliptischen Bahnen
in rastlosen Scherben der Explosion
vom unversehrten Kern ein Ahnen
in das Zurück der Fusion.

Unknown

The cosmos
a computer.

We
the operators.

The programme
unknown.

Giving Notice

Life
has leased me
a house.
A house of breath
beneath a roof
of hair.

We have a contract:
the older the house,
the higher the rent.

Soon
I will not
be able to pay it.
Soon
I must move out.

But where?

Unbekannt

Der Kosmos
ein Computer

Wir
die Operator

Das Programm
unbekannt

Kündigung

Das Leben
hat mir ein Haus
vermietet.
Ein Haus aus Atem
unter dem Dach
der Haare.

Wir haben einen Vertrag:
Je älter das Haus
desto höher die Miete.

Bald
kann ich sie
nicht mehr bezahlen.
Bald
muß ich ausziehen.

Wohin?

Cain and Abel

Abel is dead.

Cain is alive.
His successors
butcher
his successors,

till
there are no more successors
to succeed.

That is the End of the News

Everywhere
fingerprints
of catastrophes.

When we have caught
the last one in the act
there will be no mouth
to report it,
no ear to listen.

Kain und Abel

Abel ist tot.

Kain lebt.
Seine Nachkommen
erschlagen
seine Nachkommen,

bis
keine Nachkommen
mehr nachkommen.

Ende der Nachrichten

Überall
Fingerabdrücke
von Katastrophen.

Wenn wir die letzte
auf frischer Tat ertappen,
wird kein Mund mehr sein,
der berichtet,
kein Ohr, das hört.

Without a Parachute

We are all flying
in the same jet.

So don't destroy
its wings!

Parachutes are not
provided.

Future Without a Future

The stars are exhausted.
What good are the old signposts
in the skies?
From now on hell will be here
with all its own signs.

The rockets stand ready.
The countdown has started.
They will hurl
the burning torches
into the abyss above us,
a future without a future.

Ohne Fallschirm

Wir fliegen alle
im gleichen Jet.

Zerstört nicht
sein Tragwerk!

Fallschirme
gibt es nicht.

Zukunft ohne Zukunft

Die Sterne haben ausgedient.
Wozu die alten Wegweiser
über den Himmel?
Fortan wird hier die Hölle sein
mit ihren eigenen Zeichen.

Die Raketen stehen bereit.
Der Countdown läuft.
In den Abgrund über uns
schießen sie die Brandmale
der Zukunft ohne Zukunft.

Existence

This existence
without the contours
of matter

This existence
without splinters
of the Big Bang

This existence
without time and space
without beginning and end

This existence
is the *only* existence

More than Anything
(For Peter Helbich)

A breath of wind
above the wind

a gleam of light
behind the light

A pulse-beat
after the last one

over there

where there is more
than anything

Das Sein

Dieses Sein
ohne Konturen
der Materie

Dieses Sein
ohne Scherben
des Urknalls

Dieses Sein
ohne Zeit ohne Raum
ohne Anfang und Ende

Dieses Sein
ist *das Sein*

Mehr als alles
(Für Peter Hellbich)

Einen Windhauch
über dem Wind

einen Lichtschein
hinter dem Licht

einen Pulsschlag
nach dem letzten

dorthin

wo mehr ist
als alles

The Final Moment

The moment
which fails to give birth
to the next one,

the last one.

is the death
of time.

The Third Commandment

Did God rest
on the seventh day?

The news
still has not
penetrated
to the busy stars
and to the beat
of our pulse.

Der jüngste Augenblick

Der Augenblick,
der keinen nächsten
mehr gebiert,

der jüngste,

ist der Tod
der Zeit.

Das dritte Gebot

Ruhte Gott
am siebten Tag?

Bis zu seinen
fleißigen Sternen
und unserem Pulsschlag
ist die Kunde
noch nicht
gedrungen.

In the Beginning was the Dream

Dreams do not grow
on the stars,

in the expanse
of the space between them
their life darkens.

They even existed
before all that was thought,
before all that was made.

Before time and space
was the dream.

Primaeval Time

Eternity is
hard to digest.

We nourish ourselves
from its
dismembered morsels
and hunger
in the time of clocks
for the immemorial time
of eternity.

Im Anfang war der Traum

Nicht auf den Sternen
wachsen die Träume,

in den Fernen
der Zwischenräume
dunkelt ihr Leben.

Es hat sie gegeben
vor allem Gedachten,
vor allem Gemachten.

Vor Zeit und Raum
war der Traum.

Ur-Zeit

Die Ewigkeit
ist unverdaulich.

Wir nähren uns
von ihren
zerstückelten Happen
und hungern
in der Zeit der Uhren
nach der Ur-Zeit
der Ewigkeit.

Going Back

We should have strewn
pebbles
behind paradise
instead of breadcrumbs
for the birds.

Now the homesickness
between the fragments
of shattered vanities
is looking for the
way back to the source.

Presentiment

Cells
in my body,
living together
with me,
do not know
that I am
who I am.

Only when
the messengers come,
portents
of joy and pain,
do they
start
to suspect.

Zurück

Kieselsteine
hätten wir streuen sollen
hinter dem Paradies
statt Brotkrumen
für die Vögel.

Jetzt sucht das Heimweh
zwischen den Scherben
zerbrochener Eitelkeiten
den Weg
zurück in den Schoß.

Ahnung

Zellen
in meinem Körper,
mit mir zusammen
lebend,
wissen nicht,
daß ich bin,
der ich bin.

Erst wenn die
Boten kommen,
Zeichen
aus Lust und Schmerz,
dann erst
fangen sie an,
mich zu ahnen.

Typhoon

This life,
the vortex of a typhoon
hurries me
through rootless air,
urges me
in a circle around myself.

Yet somewhere within
the centre of the eye
is motionless calm,
is silence in the storm.

I circle and circle,
search and search
for the centre of the centre,
where I am, what I've been
from the beginning of things.

Asylum Seekers

We are asylum seekers
on the earth.
Our right to stay
is valid only
for a short time.

Our appeal
rejected,
we are deported,
to No-Thing-ness.

Taifun

Das Leben,
der Wirbel eines Taifuns
jagt mich
durch haltlose Luft,
treibt mich
im Kreis um mich selbst.

Doch irgendwo innen
im Zentrum des Auges
ist reglose Stille,
ist Ruhe im Sturm.

Ich kreise und kreise,
ich suche und suche
die Mitte der Mitte,
wo ich bin, was ich bin
von Anbeginn her.

Asylanten

Asylanten sind wir
auf der Erde.
Bleiberecht gilt nur
für kurze Zeit.

Abgewiesen
unsere Beschwerde.
Abgeschoben wir
zur Nicht-Ich-keit.

Death, My Friend

I will leave
the window open,
so that you
can waft in
with the night wind.
I will put out the light.
No one should see
how we greet each other.

With light fingers
you strip
the stigma of slavery
from my shoulders
and tenderly kiss
the need to breathe
from my mouth.

In your arms
you rock me to sleep
into the dreamless dream.

Tod, mein Freund

Ich werde das Fenster
geöffnet lassen,
damit du
hereinwehen kannst
mit dem Nachtwind.
Das Licht will ich löschen.
Niemand soll sehen,
wie wir uns begrüßen.

Du streifst
mit leichtem Finger
das Sklavenmal
von meinen Schultern
und küßt mir zärtlich
den Zwang zum Atemholen
vom Mund.

In deinen Armen
wiegst du mich ein
in den traumlosen Traum.

Not Entirely

He wants to be dead,
though not entirely.

A remnant of consciousness
must assure him
that he really has been freed

from sickness and pain,
from sadness and suffering,
from dejection and torment,
from revenge and war.

He wants to be dead,
though death must still
delight him.

Blackboard

And then someone came
with white chalk.
On the blackboard
he wrote the beat of my steps.
Line for line,
year for year.

Now someone is approaching
with a sponge.
He wants to erase
the writing.

All that will remain
is the board – in black.

Nicht ganz

Tot will er sein,
aber nicht ganz.

Ein Rest von Bewußtsein
soll ihm versichern,
daß er befreit ist

von Krankheit und Schmerz,
von Trauer und Leid,
von Trübsinn und Qual,
von Rache und Krieg.

Tot will er sein,
aber des Todes
will er sich freuen.

Die Tafel

Damals kam Einer
mit weißer Kreide.
Er schrieb auf die Tafel
den Takt meiner Schritte.
Zeile um Zeile,
Jahr für Jahr.

Jetzt nähert sich Einer
mit einem Schwamm.
Die Schrift
will er löschen.

Bleiben wird nur
die Tafel in Schwarz.

Dead Death

My death is dead,
for I have shot it,
her twenty-year-old mouth
exults,
laughing
through the streets.

My death is dead,
for I have shot it,
her hundred-year-old mouth
bemoans, and rattles
on the pillow.

She would love to swop,
swop
with her death.

On the Styx

The booking-office
for return tickets
on the Styx
has been closed.

It doesn't pay,
says Charon,

too few
have been sold.

Der tote Tod

Mein Tod ist tot.
Ich habe ihn erschossen,
jauchzt
ihr zwanzigjähriger Mund
lachend
durch die Straßen.

Mein Tod ist tot.
Ich habe ihn erschossen,
röchelt
ihr hundertjähriger Mund
klagend
auf dem Kissen.

Tauschen möchte sie,
tauschen
mit ihrem Tod.

Am Styx

Der Schalter
für Rückfahrkarten
am Styx
wurde geschlossen.

Es lohnt sich nicht,
sagt Charon,

zu wenige
wurden verkauft.

My Star

Of all the stars
that one single star
belongs to me.
We wave and
beckon to each other
at night
when no one
is watching.

Researchers
declare
that it is extinguished,
my star,
a thousand
times a thousand
years ago.
It no longer exists.
They say I must be wrong.

But I am not wrong.
My star and I,
we wave and
beckon to each other
night for night,
till I too am extinguished.

Mein Stern

Von allen Sternen
der eine Stern
gehört mir.
Wir blinken und
winken uns zu
nachts,
wenn niemand
uns sieht.

Die Forscher
behaupten,
er sei erloschen,
mein Stern,
vor tausend
mal tausend Jahren.
Es gibt ihn nicht mehr.
Ich müsse mich irren.

Ich irre mich nicht.
Mein Stern und ich
wir blinken und
winken uns zu
Nacht für Nacht,
bis ich erlösche.

Smoke Signals

Metamorphosis

To run away
from the creeping gait
of the caterpillar

to force open
the prison
of the larva

to rise up
on wings
towards the light

Photo

Thoughts hidden
beneath the toupet

shoulders padded
into the 'as-if'

feelings buttoned up
with the lounge-jacket

the 'I' shaken off
like dust from shoes

a flashlight
finding nothing

Metamorphose

Weglaufen
dem Kriechgang
der Raupe

aufbrechen
den Kerker
der Larve

hochsteigen
mit Flügeln
zum Licht

Foto

Gedanken versteckt
unterm Toupet

Schultern ausgestopft
ins Als-Ob

Gefühle zugeknöpft
mit dem Sakko

das Ich abgeschüttelt
als Staub von den Schultern

Blitzlicht
nicht fündig geworden

The Book

It has learned to wait.

Between paperback and leather binding
it holds its world together,
closed and concave,
in the siding
of the shelf.

It waits in expectation,
that someone might reach out for it
and bend it apart,
willing and convex,
so that it is resurrected in him
to be lived

once again.

Obituary

He had himself
served applause:
morning, afternoon and evening.

He wasn't fed enough
and yet was quite fed up.

As the cause of death
the doctor certified:
starved by a
second-hand life.

Das Buch

Es hat gelernt zu warten.

Zwischen Paperback und Leder
hält es seine Welt zusammen,
geschlossen und konkav,
auf dem Regal,
dem Abstellgleis.

Es wartet in Erwartung,
daß einer nach ihm greift,
und es sich auseinanderbiegt,
willig und konvex,
damit es in ihm aufersteht
und es gelebt wird

noch einmal.

Nachruf

Er ließ sich
Applaus servieren:
morgens, mittags, abends.

Er wurde nicht satt
und war es satt.

Als Todesursache
attestierte der Arzt:
Verhungert am Leben
aus zweiter Hand.

Computer Guided

Delete
the gossip
from the province of time
between today and today

Recall
thoughts
programmed
into the cosmos

Print
the overarching
value
in letters, syllable and word

Save
the infinite
always

The Idea

The idea —
the original text

The cosmos —
a translation

Language —
a translation of
a translation

Computergesteuert

Löschen
den Klatsch
der Zeitprovinz
zwischen heute und heute

Abrufen
Gedanken
einprogrammiert
in den Kosmos

Drucken
den überspannenden
Wert
in Buchstabe Silbe und Wort

Sichern
das zeitlose
Immer

Die Idee

Die Idee –
der Urtext

Der Kosmos –
eine Übersetzung

Die Sprache –
eine Übersetzung
einer Übersetzung

Discussion Circle

The favourite plaything
of mankind
is the ball,
said the psychologist,
and cited tennis,
football, golf
etcetera.

He smiled.

The favourite plaything
of mankind
is the ball,
his colleague
acknowledged,
and cited the earth.

He did not smile.

Career

Leapfrogging
over
bent backs

right up
to the topmost
desk

Diskussionsrunde

Das liebste Spielzeug
des Menschen
ist der Ball,
sagte der Psychologe
und verwies auf Tennis,
Fußball, Golf
und so weiter.

Er lächelte.

Das liebste Spielzeug
des Menschen
ist der Ball,
bestätigte sein Kollege
und verwies auf die Erde.

Er lächelte nicht.

Karriere

Bockspringen
über
gebeugte Rücken

hinauf
zum obersten
Schreibtisch

Smoke Signals

Signals
from summit to summit,
arising
out of burning
loneliness.

Encoded
messages
in search of
a receiver
above the shadow
of the valley.

Who?

Who is talking
when I talk,
I ask.

Who is asking
when I ask,
I wonder.

And who wonders
when I wonder?

What do I know?

Rauchzeichen

Signale
von Gipfel zu Gipfel,
aufgestiegen
aus brennender
Einsamkeit.

Verschlüsselte
Botschaften
auf der Suche
nach einem Empfänger
über dem Schatten
der Täler.

Wer?

Wer redet,
wenn ich rede,
frage ich.

Wer fragt,
wenn ich frage,
denke ich.

Wer denkt,
wenn ich denke.

Was weiß ich?

Reason

Even reason
is mortal,
I have been told.

But was it
ever born,
I asked.

A Face

Masks
   behind
      masks.

You tear them off
like the leaves of a calender,
searching
up to the last day
for a face.

Ratio

Auch Vernunft
sei sterblich,
hat man mir gesagt.

Wurde sie
je geboren,
habe ich gefragt.

Ein Gesicht

Masken
    hinter
      Masken

Du reißt sie ab
wie Kalenderblätter,
suchst
bis zum letzten Tag
ein Gesicht.

Scepticism

But I
have never
gazed into
my own eyes.

I must believe
the mirror
that they are brown.

Who knows,
perhaps it is lying.

Engaged

He has been dialling
the telephone number
of good luck.
For days, weeks, and years.

Engaged,
always engaged.

You need a bit of luck
to get through to – good luck.

Skepsis

Noch niemals
hab ich mir
in die Augen
geschaut.

Daß sie braun sind,
muß ich dem
Spiegel glauben.

Wer weiß,
ob er nicht lügt.

Besetzt

Die Rufnummer
des Glücks
hat er gewählt.
Seit Tagen, Wochen, Jahren.

Besetzt,
immer besetzt.

Glück muß man haben,
um Glück zu erreichen.

We

White mice
in the cage
of their world.

On all twos,
on all fours
along the rotating
drum in a
circle.

Surrounded
by the surrounds,
no way forward
for paws.

Winged Snail

Grant me a house,
a small house
into which
I can slip
so that I no longer
have to exist.

Grant me wings, too,
great wings,
on which
I can soar to great heights,
so that I can doubly
exist.

Wir

Weiße Mäuse
im Käfig
Welt.

Auf allen Zweien,
auf allen Vieren
die rotierende
Trommel entlang
im Kreis.

Vom Umfang
umfangen
kein Vorwärts
für Pfoten.

Flügelschnecke

Schenk mir ein Haus,
ein kleines Haus,
damit ich
hineinschlüpfen kann,
um nicht mehr
zu sein.

Schenk mir doch Flügel,
weite Flügel,
damit ich
mich aufschwingen kann,
um doppelt
zu sein.

No Difference

He was asked:
Allah or Yahweh?
He said: God.

He was asked:
Croat or Serb?
He said: Man.

Sisyphus

Scientists have managed
to overcome
gravity
with the greatest success.

They have been
completely unsuccessful
in overcoming
egoism.

They are still exploring it.

Have they never heard
of Sisyphus?

Kein Unterschied

Er wurde gefragt:
Allah oder Jahve?
Er sagte: Gott.

Er wurde gefragt:
Kroate oder Serbe?
Er sagte: Mensch.

Sisyphus

Die Überwindung
der Schwerkraft
gelang den Forschern
äußerst erfolgreich.

Die Überwindung
des Egoismus
erforschen sie
völlig erfolglos.

Sie forschen weiter.

Ist ihnen
Sisyphos nicht bekannt?

Freedom

As free as the sea
which pitches and tosses
its tides between the
continents,

as free as the swallow
shuttling
from homeland to homeland,

as free as the tulip,
silently closing the door
on the night,

that's how free I am.

Put on Ice

His dreams
lie frozen
in the deepfreeze
with five stars.
Here no corruption
can reach them.
Decay remains
locked out.

His dreams
are eternally green,
eternally unlived.

Freiheit

So frei wie das Meer,
das seine Gezeiten
zwischen den Kontinenten
schaukelt,

so frei wie die Schwalbe
im Pendelflug
von Heimat zu Heimat,

so frei wie die Tulpe,
lautlos die Türe schließend
vor der Nacht,

so frei bin ich.

Auf Eis gelegt

Seine Träume
liegen eingefroren
im Kühlfach
mit fünf Sternen.
Hier erreicht sie
keine Fäulnis.
Verwesung
bleibt ausgesperrt.

Ewig grün
sind seine Träume,
ewig ungelebt.

Bibliography

Poetry
1979 *The Other Shore*, Vienna (out of print)
1981 *Under my Eyelids*, 1st edition, Waldbrunn
1981 *Waterfall of Time* (out of print)
1983 *I Cannot Live with Less*, Waldbrunn
1985 *Netopyri mlceni (Silence of Bats)*, Prague
1986 *Unreachably Near*, Eisingen
1986 *A Ray of Your Light*, Munich
1987 2nd Edition
1988 *Co mi spi v noci pod vicky*, Prague
1989 *Nedosazitelne blizko*, Prague
1990 *Under my Eyelids*, 2nd enlarged edition, Eisingen
1991 *In the Land of Hours*, Konstanz
1992 *Life is a Circle*, Konstanz
1992 *Only When the Messengers Come*, Eisingen
1994 *Under my Eyelids*, English translation, London
1994 *Time is a Circle*, Konstanz
1994 *Poems*, arabic translation, Beirut, Lebanon
1995 *Under my Eyelids*, 3rd edition, Eisingen

Prose
1990 *In the Shadow of Prague*

Translations into German
1982 Jaroslav Seifert:
   In the Mirror he has Darkness, Waldbrunn
1985 *What Was Once Love*, Hanau
1986 Poetry in: *A Sky Full of Ravens*, Munich
1987 Nezval, Poems in: *Toyen*, Frankfurt am Main
1995 *Ivan Divis*, Sursum, Eisingen

Other German Titles Published by Forest Books

PIED POETS
Contemporary Verse of the Transylvanian and Danube Germans of Romania
Edited and translated by Robert Elsie
DUAL TEXT ENGLISH/GERMAN

A somewhat frivolous poetic tombstone! Pied Poets marks the passing of the 'fifth German literature', that of the German minority of Romania.

ISBN 0-948259-77-9   208 pages   paper £8.95   1990
Illustrated by Silke Ulbricht

ANTHOLOGY OF SORBIAN POETRY FROM THE 16TH–20TH CENTURIES
Edited and translated by Robert Elsie
(Contains sample of original language)

The Sorbs are a Slavic minority in what was recently East Germany and this is the first translation of their work into English.

UNESCO COLLECTION OF REPRESENTATIVE WORKS
European Series

ISBN 0-948259-72-8   96 pages   paper £6.95   1990
Illustrated by Silke Ulbricht

Step Human into this World
Travel Poems by Olav Münzberg
Translated from the German by
Mitch Cohen and Ingrid Stoll
Introduced by Hans Christoph Buch

From the fall of the Berlin wall to Tianamen Square, we are taken on a journey that expresses solidarity with the poor and the oppressed.

ISBN 0-948259-53-1   144 pages   paper £8.95   1991

Heinz Piontek
Selected Poems
Translated by Ewald Osers

A lyrical poet whose work reflects the reactions of a generation which witnessed the collapse of the Third Reich and which matured under the new order.

ISBN 1-85610-033-2   96 pages   paper £6.95   1994

Under My Eyelids
Poems of
Olly Komenda-Soentgerath
Translated by Tom Beck
Afterword by Jaroslav Seifert

Lyrical poems with a glowing urgency. A Czech-German poet who has won many literary awards.

ISBN 1-85610-037-5   96 pages   paper £6.95   1994

YOUNG POETS OF GERMANY
Translated by Raymond Hargreaves
Edited by Uwe-Michael Gutzschhahn

An anthology from East and West. 27 poets born between 1952 and 1962. Wry, laconic, full of a sense of loss or deprivation, these diverse and dissenting voices are characterised by a feeling of displacement and dislocation.

UNESCO COLLECTION OF REPRESENTATIVE WORKS
European Series
ISBN 1-85610-032-4   190 pages   paper £10.95   1994